Prayers for My Family

DATE   NAME

Be Still and Know That I'm With You...
Psalm 46:10

Prayers for Myself

DATE	REFLECTIONS

Prayers For My Friends

DATE   **NAMES**

For with God, nothing is impossible...

Prayers For my loves

DATE   NAME

My Prayer

Prayer JOURNAL

Spiritual Inspiration

" I can do All
THINGS
through
CHRIST
WHO STRENGTHENS ME "

- PHILIPPIANS 4:13 -

Sermon JOURNAL

WHAT I LEARNED TODAY

Notes:

"The of GOD my ROCK in Him will I TRUST"

- 2 SAMUEL 22:3 -

Sermon JOURNAL

WHAT I LEARNED TODAY

Notes:

" I will walk by
FAITH
even when I can't
SEE "

- 2 CORINTHIANS 5:1 -

Sermon JOURNAL

WHAT I LEARNED TODAY

Notes:

" Be Still
in the Presence
OF THE **LORD**
and wait patiently
for him to act. "

- PSALM 37:7 -

Sermon JOURNAL

WHAT I LEARNED TODAY

Notes:

"I Praise You BECAUSE I AM fearfully and wonderfully MADE"

- PSALM 134:14 -

Sermon JOURNAL

WHAT I LEARNED TODAY

Notes:

" Be Not Afraid, ONLY BELIEVE "

- MARK 5:36 -

I AM GRATEFUL FOR

Sermon JOURNAL

WHAT I LEARNED TODAY

Notes:

" *By his wounds*
WE ARE **HEALED** "

- ISAIAH 53:5 -

I AM GRATEFUL FOR

Prayer Requests

DATE	NAMES

Prayer Card

Prayer Card

Hymn Study

HYMN:

Favorite Verse

Lyrics of Faith

Sing to him, Sing praise to him, tell of all his wonderful acts.
Psalm 105:2

sermon NOTES

DATE / / **TOPIC:**

SPEAKER: **PLACE OF WORSHIP:**

SCRIPTURE **NOTES**

Key Points

sermon TRACKER

DATE

SCRIPTURE

NOTES

Reflections

DATE

Today's stand-out verse:

I am thankful for:

Prayer Requests:

Inspirational Scripture:

sermon NOTES

DATE / / **TOPIC**

Scripture

Prayer & Praise

Personal Reflections

sermon NOTES

DATE / /

SERMON

Scripture

Notes

Be on your guard; stand firm in the faith; be courageous; be strong.
1 Corinthians 4:16-18

Sermon NOTES

DATE / /   **TOPIC:**

SPEAKER: **PLACE OF WORSHIP:**

Key Points

In GOD we trust

DATE:

This week I will focus on:

What I am most grateful for:

In GOD *we trust*

DATE:

This week I was most blessed by:

My calling in life is:

In GOD we trust

DATE:

My favorite passage of scripture is:

God is leading me to make the following changes:

In GOD we trust

DATE:

I feel God's presence most when:

What brings me the most joy is:

DATE:

My spiritual gifts are:

My enthusiasm for the gospel is increased when:

In GOD we trust

DATE:

One way I can apply the gospel to my life is:

An act of obedience God is prompting me to take is:

My time with the LORD

DATE:

Scripture that inspired me today:

Dear Lord:

"...but by my
STRENGTH
by His"

—2 Corinthians 12:9

" Be Still
in the Presence
of the **LORD**
and wait patiently
for him to act. "

- PSALM 37:7 -

"I will not be SHAKEN"

- PSALM 16:8 -

" FOLLOW YOUR
faith
and he'll lead
THE WAY "

Prayers for My Family

DATE   **NAME**

Be Still and Know That I'm With You...
Psalm 46:10

Prayers for Myself

DATE

REFLECTIONS

Prayers For My Friends

DATE	NAMES

For with God, nothing is impossible...

Prayers For my loves

DATE   **NAME**

My Prayer

Prayer JOURNAL

PERSONAL REFLECTIONS

Spiritual Inspiration

" I can do All
THINGS
through
CHRIST
who STRENGTHENS ME "

- PHILIPPIANS 4:13 -

Sermon JOURNAL

WHAT I LEARNED TODAY

Notes:

" The of. GOD
my ROCK
in Him will
I TRUST "

- 2 SAMUEL 22:3 -

Sermon JOURNAL

WHAT I LEARNED TODAY

Notes:

" I will walk by
FAITH
even when I can't
SEE "

- 2 CORINTHIANS 5:1 -

Sermon JOURNAL

WHAT I LEARNED TODAY

Notes:

" Be Still
in the Presence
of the LORD
and wait patiently
for him to act. "

- PSALM 37:7 -

Sermon JOURNAL

WHAT I LEARNED TODAY

Notes:

" I Praise You
I AM BECAUSE
fearfully and wonderfully
MADE "

- PSALM 134:14 -

Sermon JOURNAL

WHAT I LEARNED TODAY

Notes:

" *Be Not Afraid,*
ONLY **BELIEVE** "

- MARK 5:36 -

I AM GRATEFUL FOR

Sermon JOURNAL

WHAT I LEARNED TODAY

Notes:

" *By his wounds*
WE ARE **HEALED** "

- ISAIAH 53:5 -

I AM GRATEFUL FOR

Prayer Requests

DATE   **NAMES**

Prayer Card   *Prayer Card*

Hymn Study

HYMN:

Favorite Verse

Lyrics of Faith

Sing to him, Sing praise to him, tell of all his wonderful acts.
Psalm 105:2

sermon NOTES

DATE / /   **TOPIC:**

SPEAKER: **PLACE OF WORSHIP:**

SCRIPTURE   **NOTES**

Key Points

sermon TRACKER

DATE

SCRIPTURE

NOTES

Reflections

DATE

Today's stand-out verse:

I am thankful for:

Prayer Requests:

Inspirational Scripture:

sermon NOTES

DATE / /   **TOPIC**

Scripture

Prayer & Praise

Personal Reflections

sermon NOTES

DATE

SERMON

Scripture

Notes

Be on your guard; stand firm in the faith; be courageous; be strong.
1 Corinthians 4:16-18

Sermon NOTES

DATE / /   **TOPIC:**

SPEAKER: **PLACE OF WORSHIP:**

Key Points

In GOD we trust

DATE:

This week I will focus on:

What I am most grateful for:

In GOD we trust

DATE:

This week I was most blessed by:

My calling in life is:

In GOD we trust

DATE:

My favorite passage of scripture is:

God is leading me to make the following changes:

In GOD we trust

DATE:

I feel God's presence most when:

What brings me the most joy is:

DATE:

My spiritual gifts are:

My enthusiasm for the gospel is increased when:

DATE:

One way I can apply the gospel to my life is:

An act of obedience God is prompting me to take is:

My time with the LORD

DATE:

Scripture that inspired me today:

Dear Lord:

"Not by My STRENGTH, by His"

- Zechariah 4:6 -

" Be Still
in the Presence
of the **LORD**
and wait patiently
for him to act. "

- PSALM 37:7 -

"I will not be SHAKEN"

- PSALM 16:8 -

" FOLLOW YOUR
faith
and he'll lead
THE WAY "

Prayers for My Family

DATE   NAME

Be Still and Know That I'm With You...
Psalm 46:10

Prayers for Myself

DATE	REFLECTIONS

Prayers For My Friends

DATE   NAMES

For with God, nothing is impossible…

Prayers For my loves

DATE   **NAME**

My Prayer

Prayer JOURNAL

PERSONAL REFLECTIONS

Spiritual Inspiration

" I can do All THINGS through CHRIST WHO STRENGTHENS ME "

- PHILIPPIANS 4:13 -

Sermon JOURNAL

WHAT I LEARNED TODAY

Notes:

" The of GOD
my ROCK
in Him will
I TRUST "

- 2 SAMUEL 22:3 -

Sermon JOURNAL

WHAT I LEARNED TODAY

Notes:

" I will walk by
FAITH
even when I can't
SEE "

- 2 CORINTHIANS 5:1 -

Sermon JOURNAL

WHAT I LEARNED TODAY

Notes:

" Be Still
in the Presence
of the LORD
and wait patiently
for him to act. "

- PSALM 37:7 -

Sermon JOURNAL

WHAT I LEARNED TODAY

Notes:

" I Praise You
I AM BECAUSE
fearfully and wonderfully
MADE "

- PSALM 134:14 -

Sermon JOURNAL

WHAT I LEARNED TODAY

Notes:

" Be Not Afraid, ONLY BELIEVE "

- MARK 5:36 -

I AM GRATEFUL FOR

Sermon JOURNAL

WHAT I LEARNED TODAY

Notes:

" By his wounds

WE ARE **HEALED** "

- ISAIAH 53:5 -

I AM GRATEFUL FOR

Prayer Requests

DATE   **NAMES**

Prayer Card

Prayer Card

Hymn Study

HYMN:

Favorite Verse

Lyrics of Faith

Sing to him, Sing praise to him, tell of all his wonderful acts.
Psalm 105:2

sermon NOTES

DATE / /   **TOPIC:**

SPEAKER: **PLACE OF WORSHIP:**

SCRIPTURE   **NOTES**

Key Points

sermon TRACKER

DATE

SCRIPTURE

NOTES

Reflections

Today's stand-out verse:

I am thankful for:

Prayer Requests:

Inspirational Scripture:

sermon NOTES

DATE / / **TOPIC**

Scripture

Prayer & Praise

Personal Reflections

sermon NOTES

DATE / /

SERMON

Scripture

Notes

Be on your guard; stand firm in the faith; be courageous; be strong.
1 Corinthians 4:16-18

Sermon NOTES

DATE / /   TOPIC:

SPEAKER: PLACE OF WORSHIP:

Key Points

In GOD we trust

DATE:

This week I will focus on:

What I am most grateful for:

In GOD *we trust*

DATE:

This week I was most blessed by:

My calling in life is:

DATE:

My favorite passage of scripture is:

God is leading me to make the following changes:

In **GOD** *we trust*

DATE:

I feel God's presence most when:

What brings me the most joy is:

DATE:

My spiritual gifts are:

My enthusiasm for the gospel is increased when:

In GOD we trust

DATE:

One way I can apply the gospel to my life is:

An act of obedience God is prompting me to take is:

My time with the LORD

DATE:

Scripture that inspired me today:

Dear Lord:

"Not by my
STRENGTH,
by His"

– Zechariah 4:6 –

" Be Still
in the Presence
of the **LORD**
and wait patiently
for him to act. "

- PSALM 37:7 -

"I will not be SHAKEN"

- PSALM 16:8 -

" FOLLOW YOUR
faith
and he'll lead
THE WAY **"**

Prayers for My Family

DATE NAME

Be Still and Know That I'm With You...
Psalm 46:10

Prayers for Myself

DATE   REFLECTIONS

Prayers For My Friends

DATE	NAMES

For with God, nothing is impossible...

Prayers For my loves

DATE   **NAME**

My Prayer

Prayer JOURNAL

PERSONAL REFLECTIONS

Spiritual Inspiration

" I can do All
THINGS
through
CHRIST
WHO STRENGTHENS ME "

- PHILIPPIANS 4:13 -

Sermon JOURNAL

WHAT I LEARNED TODAY

Notes:

" The *of* GOD my ROCK in Him will I TRUST "

- 2 SAMUEL 22:3 -

Sermon JOURNAL

WHAT I LEARNED TODAY

Notes:

" I will walk by
FAITH
even when I can't
SEE "

- 2 CORINTHIANS 5:1 -

DATE / /

Sermon JOURNAL

WHAT I LEARNED TODAY

Notes:

" Be Still
in the Presence
of the **LORD**
and wait patiently
for him to act. "

- PSALM 37:7 -

DATE / /

Sermon JOURNAL

WHAT I LEARNED TODAY

Notes:

" I Praise You

I AM **BECAUSE**

fearfully and wonderfully

MADE "

- PSALM 134:14 -

Sermon JOURNAL

WHAT I LEARNED TODAY

Notes:

" Be Not Afraid, ONLY BELIEVE "

- MARK 5:36 -

I AM GRATEFUL FOR

Sermon JOURNAL

WHAT I LEARNED TODAY

Notes:

" By his wounds
WE ARE HEALED "
- ISAIAH 53:5 -

I AM GRATEFUL FOR

Prayer Requests

DATE   NAMES

Prayer Card   Prayer Card

Hymn Study

HYMN:

Favorite Verse

Lyrics of Faith

Sing to him, Sing praise to him, tell of all his wonderful acts.
Psalm 105:2

sermon NOTES

DATE / /   TOPIC:

SPEAKER: PLACE OF WORSHIP:

SCRIPTURE   NOTES

Key Points

sermon TRACKER

DATE

SCRIPTURE

NOTES

Reflections